Suhana Rossi

Cartagena Travel Guide

Title: Cartagena Travel Guide
Author: Suhana Rossi
Published by: NEXTUNICORN PUBLISHER PROPRIETORSHIP
Publisher's Address: Shree Dwarkadhish Ji Ka Was, Emri, Rajsamand, RAJASTHAN, India. Pincode: 313342
Printer Details: Published online on various platforms.
Edition: 01
ISBN: 978-81-968207-8-7

Images Source: Pixbay: (https://pixabay.com/)

Disclaimer: The author and publisher disclaim all liability for accuracy, loss, or damage arising from the use of this travel guide; users are urged to independently verify information and prioritize personal safety.

Catalog

Welcome to Cartagena 1
Cartagena's 12 Must-Visit Destinations 3
    1. San Felipe Castle (Castillo San Felipe de Barajas): 3
    2. Getsemaní Neighborhood: 4
    3. Rosario Islands: 6
    4. Convento de la Popa: 7
    5. Cartagena Cathedral: 8
    6. Lighthouse Cartagena Colombia: 9
    7. Teatro Romano de Cartagena: 10
    8. Cartagena Town Square Facade: 11
    9. Monumento Torre del Reloj: 12
    10. Alcaldía Mayor de Cartagena de Indias: 13
    11. Fuerte de San Fernando de Bocachica: 14
    12. Playa De Bocagrande: 15
Need to Know 17
Currency: 17
Language: 17
Room Tax: 17
Emergency Numbers: 17
Daily Costs: 17
Opening Hours: 18
Arriving in Cartagena: 18
Itineraries 19
Adventure Activities in Cartagena 21
A brief History 25
List of 10 Hotels in Cartagena 29
Visas and Residency in Cartagena 31
1. Entry for European Citizens: 31
2. Visa Exemptions for Select Countries: 31
3. Visas for Non-Colombian Nationals: 31
4. Residence and Work for Expatriates: 31
5. Permanent Residence for Foreign Citizens: 31
Travelling to Cartagena 33
By Air: 33
Entering the Country: 33
By Land: 33
By Bus: 33
By Car and Motorcycle: 33
By Train: 33
By Sea: 34

Welcome to the captivating city of Cartagena, where history and charm intertwine to create a vibrant cultural tapestry. As you wander through its streets and visit its historic sites, you'll be immersed in a world of perplexity and burstiness. While Paris may capture attention with its allure, Cartagena's unique blend of colonial architecture and contemporary artistry sets it apart. This city is a true testament to its historical significance, with remnants of Spanish colonial influence that tell a compelling narrative.

Begin your exploration in Old Town, where the cobbled streets transport you back in time to the colonial era. Marvel at the majestic San Felipe Castle, a fortress that once guarded against pirates, and take in the vibrant atmosphere of Plaza Santo Domingo. The fusion of Spanish and Caribbean influences creates an enchanting cultural mosaic that captivates every visitor.

Venture into Getsemaní, an eclectic neighborhood known for its colorful street art that brings Cartagena's past and present to life. Immerse yourself in the local atmosphere as you stroll through Plaza de la Trinidad, surrounded by lively cafes and the rhythmic beats of Afro-Caribbean music. The juxtaposition of historic charm and contemporary creativity makes Getsemaní a must-visit cultural hub.

Experience modern elegance in Bocagrande, where upscale hotels, sleek skyscrapers, and pristine beaches await. While contrasting with the historic heart of Cartagena, Bocagrande adds sophistication to the city's cultural repertoire. Indulge in luxurious amenities, dine at world-class restaurants, and bask in the golden sunshine on the shores.

Cartagena's culinary scene is a symphony of flavors that blends traditional Colombian dishes with international influences. In Old Town, street vendors offer gastronomic delights such as arepas and empanadas that will tantalize your taste buds as you meander through charming alleys. For a more refined dining experience, Bocagrande boasts fine establishments that showcase the city's gastronomic prowess, serving seafood delights and innovative fusion dishes that will delight your senses.

Beyond its cultural treasures and culinary delights, Cartagena's coastal beauty is truly captivating. The city is blessed with diverse landscapes, from serene beaches to lush mangroves, inviting you to explore the wonders of nature.

Escape to the nearby Rosario Islands, where turquoise waters and pristine beaches create a tropical paradise. Snorkel in coral reefs, relax on secluded shores, and immerse yourself in the natural beauty that defines the Caribbean coast.

Embark on mangrove ecotours in La Boquilla and discover the rich wildlife that thrives in its dense forests. Paddle through intricate waterways and marvel at the ecological marvels that contribute to Cartagena's environmental richness.

Cartagena offers a wide range of outdoor adventures that complement its cultural and culinary offerings. Whether you're exploring historic streets, indulging in local delicacies, or immersing yourself in coastal beauty, this city invites you to discover the depth of its cultural and natural wonders.

1. San Felipe Castle (Castillo San Felipe de Barajas):

San Felipe Castle, a formidable fortress built in the 17th century, has a rich history filled with battles and its role as a crucial defensive structure during invasions. The castle offers an array of attractions for visitors to explore. From the intricate system of tunnels and underground chambers to the strategic defense points and breathtaking panoramic views of Cartagena, there is much to discover.

To fully experience San Felipe Castle, it is recommended to visit during the morning or late afternoon to avoid the scorching heat. The castle operates from 8:00 AM to 6:00 PM on a daily basis.

For those seeking hidden gems within the castle, venturing into the tunnels will unveil hidden chambers that provide insight into its historical significance. Additionally, don't miss out on experiencing authentic Colombian snacks by trying local street food vendors located nearby.

If you have any inquiries or need further information about San Felipe Castle, feel free to contact us at +57 5 6601571.

Embark on an unforgettable journey through time at San Felipe Castle and immerse yourself in its captivating stories while savoring delectable culinary delights along the way.

Getsemaní, a once humble residential area for the working class, has undergone a remarkable transformation into a thriving cultural epicenter. It has managed to retain its historical allure while embracing a vibrant artistic energy.

There are several key attractions in Getsemaní that are worth exploring. One of the highlights is the captivating street art that adorns the neighborhood's walls, showcasing an array of visually striking and thought-provoking artwork. Additionally, Plaza de la Trinidad offers a lively atmosphere where locals and visitors alike can immerse themselves in the vibrant spirit of the community. Another must-visit spot is the iconic "La India Catalina" monument, which holds great historical significance.

To truly experience the essence of Getsemaní, it is recommended to visit in the evening when the neighborhood comes alive with its dynamic nightlife. The streets are filled with energy as people gather to enjoy live music performances, indulge in delicious food from street vendors, and engage in lively conversations.

As for opening hours, since Getsemaní is primarily a residential area rather than a specific attraction or establishment, there are no set hours of operation. However, it's important to note that individual attractions within Getsemaní may have their own schedules that visitors should be mindful of.

If you plan to explore Getsemaní, it is best to do so independently. This allows you to wander freely through its intriguing alleys and stumble upon hidden gems such as undiscovered street art masterpieces and charming local cafes. These hidden gems offer an authentic glimpse into the neighborhood's culture and provide unique experiences that cannot be found elsewhere.

When it comes to culinary delights, Getsemaní does not disappoint. The neighborhood boasts numerous local eateries where you can savor traditional Colombian dishes like mouthwatering arepas and savory empanadas. These culinary delights showcase the rich flavors and diverse gastronomy that Colombia has to offer.

In conclusion, visiting Getsemaní is a journey that takes you through a neighborhood steeped in history and brimming with artistic expression. By immersing yourself in its vibrant atmosphere, exploring hidden gems, and indulging in local cuisine, you will create lasting memories of an authentic Colombian experience.

The Rosario Islands, located off the coast of Cartagena, have a rich history dating back centuries. They have served as a sanctuary for pirates and a source of inspiration for artists. When visiting these islands, you can look forward to a variety of attractions that highlight their natural beauty and diverse marine life. Immerse yourself in the tranquility of pristine beaches, dive into vibrant coral reefs while snorkeling, and discover the fascinating underwater world. One must-visit spot is Playa Blanca, known for its powdery white sand that will leave you in awe. To make the most of your trip, it's recommended to plan your visit between December and March when the weather is at its best and beach conditions are ideal. The islands do not have specific opening hours; however, boat tours typically depart in the morning allowing you to explore these stunning destinations at your own pace. If you're interested in exploring further or need assistance with island tours, feel free to reach out to tour operators who specialize in this area. As you venture beyond the well-known spots, don't forget to uncover the hidden gems among these islands. These lesser-known islands offer quieter beaches and provide more intimate experiences away from bustling crowds. And when it comes to satisfying your taste buds, indulge in fresh seafood delicacies at beachside restaurants that showcase the vibrant flavors of Caribbean cuisine

---

4. Convento de la Popa:

Convento de la Popa, a symbol of colonial religious influence dating back to the 17th century, offers visitors breathtaking views of Cartagena. When exploring this historical site, you can visit the chapel, take in the serene courtyard, and marvel at panoramic vistas of the city and the Caribbean Sea. For photography enthusiasts, it is recommended to visit in the morning or late afternoon when lighting conditions are optimal. The convent is open daily from 8:00 AM to 6:00 PM. If you need any further information or assistance during your visit, you can reach out to them at +57 5 6642466.

To truly uncover hidden gems within Convento de la Popa, venture into its lesser-known corners where you'll find tranquil spots boasting remarkable views. Additionally, for a delightful culinary experience paired with stunning scenery, consider visiting nearby cafes that offer refreshing drinks.

Cartagena Cathedral, a magnificent piece of Spanish colonial architecture dating back to the 16th century, bears witness to centuries of religious and cultural events. Its grandeur and intricate altar, along with its collection of historic religious artifacts, are key attractions for visitors. For a more serene experience, it is advisable to visit the cathedral in the morning. The opening hours vary, with specific timings allocated for religious services. To get in touch, you can reach them at +57 5 6646070. In addition to its architectural beauty, attending a religious service at the cathedral offers a unique cultural experience that should not be missed. To further enhance your visit, explore the nearby cafes and restaurants that offer a delightful combination of historic charm and contemporary cuisine.

The Cartagena Lighthouse, an iconic maritime landmark that has guided ships for centuries, holds a captivating past in aiding navigation throughout the Caribbean. Ascend to its pinnacle for breathtaking panoramic vistas of both the city and the vast expanse of the sea. Immerse yourself in the lighthouse's rich maritime heritage as you peruse informative exhibits that shed light on its significance.

To truly appreciate the captivating allure of this historical site, timing your visit during sunset provides a picturesque backdrop that will leave you spellbound. However, if you seek crystal-clear views, daytime visits are recommended.

Plan your visit accordingly as the lighthouse welcomes visitors daily from 9:00 AM to 5:00 PM. Should you require any further information or have inquiries, feel free to reach out via telephone at +57 5 6601571.

For those with an adventurous spirit, exploring the surrounding area unveils hidden gems in the form of lesser-known viewpoints offering unique perspectives and stunning vistas.

Indulge your senses in culinary delights at nearby cafes that boast a relaxed ambiance perfect for savoring local snacks while immersing yourself in maritime views that never fail to captivate.

---

7. Teatro Romano de Cartagena:

The Roman Theatre of Cartagena, with its ancient roots dating back to the 1st century BC, is a captivating piece of history that showcases the city's significance during the Roman era. This architectural marvel, the well-preserved Roman amphitheater, not only serves as a testament to the past but also plays host to occasional cultural events and performances that immerse visitors in its historical ambiance.

For those planning a visit, it is recommended to explore this archaeological site during daytime hours when natural lighting accentuates its beauty. The theater is open daily from 10:00 AM to 6:00 PM, providing ample time for an enriching experience.

To get in touch or gather more information about this remarkable attraction, you can contact them at +57 5 6601571. Additionally, don't miss out on hidden gems awaiting discovery within the theater. Attending a cultural event or performance will transport you back in time and allow you to fully appreciate its historical significance.

After immersing yourself in history, indulge your taste buds with Mediterranean-inspired cuisine at nearby restaurants. These culinary delights provide a perfect way to round off your visit and make it truly memorable.

---

8. Cartagena Town Square Facade:

Cartagena's town squares, with their colonial facades, serve as a testament to the city's rich history as a hub of trade and culture. These squares offer an array of attractions, each boasting its own unique charm and vibrant atmosphere. Visitors can wander through the bustling markets, surrounded by colorful facades, and soak in the local culture.

For an authentic experience, it is recommended to visit in the evening when both locals and tourists gather in these squares. The squares are open throughout the day, with specific hours dedicated to the markets. Exploring independently allows you to uncover hidden gems such as hidden courtyards and small shops tucked away behind the facades.

Indulge your taste buds with local street food and savor alfresco dining in these vibrant squares. Immerse yourself in Cartagena's culinary delights while enjoying the lively ambiance. The combination of historical significance, hidden treasures, and mouthwatering cuisine make these town squares a must-visit destination for any traveler.

---

9. Monumento Torre del Reloj:

The Clock Tower, an emblem of Cartagena's entrance, has graced the landscape since the 18th century, extending a warm welcome to visitors of the historic Old Town. It serves as a key attraction, captivating onlookers with its iconic structure and beckoning them to venture into the enchanting realm of the Old Town. You can visit at any time, but there is something truly magical about experiencing it in the evening when the city awakens with a mesmerizing display of lights. The Clock Tower remains accessible around the clock, allowing you to explore at your own pace. For those seeking hidden gems, scaling the nearby city walls offers an opportunity for additional panoramic views of both the city and the glistening Caribbean Sea. To tantalize your taste buds, there are an array of nearby cafes and restaurants that promise culinary delights and unforgettable dining experiences.

---

10. Alcaldía Mayor de Cartagena de Indias:

The Mayor's Office in Cartagena is a testament to the city's rich history and architectural heritage. It serves as the local government and is housed in a building that showcases the colonial charm of Cartagena.

One of the main attractions in the area is the Mayor's Office itself, with its stunning historic architecture. Visitors can also explore the nearby Plaza de la Aduana, which provides a picturesque backdrop to the office building.

For those interested in experiencing local governance firsthand, it is recommended to visit on weekdays during office hours. This will give you a glimpse into how things are run at a local level.

As for opening hours, you can expect the Mayor's Office to be open during regular business hours, just like any other government office.

If you prefer to explore independently, there are no restrictions on visiting and taking in the sights at your own pace.

To truly immerse yourself in the local culture and gain insights into daily life, make sure to engage with locals who frequent the plaza. They can provide valuable information and stories about their experiences living in Cartagena.

Lastly, don't miss out on the culinary delights that surround the Mayor's Office. There are plenty of cafes where you can enjoy traditional Colombian cuisine while observing local customs and traditions. It's an excellent way to embrace both food and culture simultaneously.

11. Fuerte de San Fernando de Bocachica:

The fortress on Tierrabomba Island, constructed in the 18th century, holds a significant role in protecting Cartagena from naval attacks throughout history. It boasts well-preserved military architecture, cannons, and strategic vantage points that offer breathtaking views of the Caribbean Sea. To fully appreciate this historical gem, it is recommended to visit in the morning to beat the heat. Additionally, occasional events may feature captivating historical reenactments that transport visitors back in time. The fortress operates daily from 9:00 AM to 5:00 PM for exploration. For further information or inquiries, you can reach out via telephone at +57 5 6601571. Delve deeper into the fort's intriguing past by taking a guided tour that uncovers hidden tunnels and reveals fascinating stories about its history. After immersing yourself in all the historical wonders, don't forget to indulge in culinary delights during your visit. You can either pack a picnic or savor local seafood at one of the charming beachside restaurants located on Tierrabomba Island

---

12. Playa De Bocagrande:

Bocagrande's beach, with its mesmerizing expanse of golden sands, has long been a sanctuary for both locals and tourists seeking solace from the bustling cityscape. This idyllic coastal retreat offers a tranquil escape where one can bask in the warmth of the sun, immerse themselves in the azure waters, or simply luxuriate on the scenic shoreline.

Whether you're an adrenaline junkie craving exhilarating water sports or yearning for a serene respite to unwind and rejuvenate, this captivating beach has something for everyone. From thrilling aquatic adventures to blissful moments of relaxation, Bocagrande's beach promises an unforgettable experience.

For those seeking a more serene ambiance, weekdays offer a quieter atmosphere where you can indulge in uninterrupted serenity. However, if you prefer a livelier ambiance with vibrant beachside activities and festivities, weekends are perfect for immersing yourself in the energetic vibe that permeates this coastal paradise.

The allure of Bocagrande's beach knows no bounds as it remains accessible throughout the day, allowing visitors to revel in its splendor from dawn till dusk. Whether you prefer early morning strolls along the shore or romantic moonlit walks under the starry sky, this ethereal destination caters to all your desires.

When it comes to exploring this enchanting locale, independent exploration is highly encouraged. Venture beyond the beaten path and uncover hidden gems nestled amidst secluded stretches of sand that lie beyond the reaches of mainstream tourism. These hidden treasures offer solitude and tranquility for those seeking an intimate connection with nature.

Indulge your taste buds in a culinary extravaganza as beachside vendors tantalize your senses with an array of delectable snacks that reflect local flavors. For those craving a more refined dining experience, nearby restaurants beckon with their fusion of exquisite local delicacies and tantalizing international cuisine. Embark on a gastronomic journey that will leave you craving for more.

Here's what you need to know about Cartagena:

Currency:

- In Cartagena, the official currency is the Colombian Peso (COP).

Language:

- Spanish is the official language in Cartagena.

Room Tax:

- Visitors should be aware of potential room occupancy taxes that might be charged by local accommodations. Check with your specific lodgings for details on any applicable fees.

Emergency Numbers:

- In case of emergencies in Cartagena, remember these vital contact numbers:
  - Ambulance: 123
  - Police: 112
  - Fire: 119
- When calling from outside Colombia, dial your international access code, followed by Colombia's country code (%57), and then the number (including the '0').

Daily Costs:

Budget (Less than COP 200,000):

- Budget travelers can find affordable options in Cartagena. Hostel dorm beds typically range from COP 30,000 to COP 60,000, while budget hotel rooms can be found for COP 80,000 to COP 150,000. Local eateries offer meals ranging from COP 10,000 to COP 25,000.

Midrange (COP 200,000–COP 500,000):

- Midrange options provide good value in Cartagena. Double rooms in midrange hotels typically cost between COP 150,000 and COP 300,000. Dining at local restaurants averages around COP50 ,00 to C OP100 ,00 per meal.

Top End (More than COP500 ,00):

- Luxury travelers can indulge in premium experiences. Four-or five-star hotel rooms range from CO P400 ,00 to CO P700 ,00 . Fine dining experiences may cost between CO P150 ,00 and CO P300 ,00 per person.

Opening Hours:

- Cartagena's opening hours can vary based on the season:

  - Banks: 8:00 AM–12:00 PM and 2:00 PM–6:00 PM, Monday to Friday

  - Restaurants: 12:00 PM–3:00 PM and 7:00 PM–11:00 PM

  - Cafes: 7:00 AM–8:00 PM

  - Bars and clubs :8 :0 0PM –4 :0 0AM

  - Shops :9 :0 0AM –1 :0 0PM and3 :0 0PM –7 :0 OP M, Monday to Saturday

Arriving in Cartagena:

- Depending on your arrival point, consider these transportation options:

  - Rafael Núñez International Airport:Taxis are readily available, with a fare of approximately COP20 ,000 to CO P30 ,000 to the city center. Alternatively, airport shuttles offer convenient transfers.

With these practical details, you're well-equipped to navigate Cartagena with confidence, immersing yourself in its vibrant culture, history, and coastal beauty.

Cartagena Escapade - A Journey of Historic Marvels, Coastal Charms, and Cultural Riches

Embark on a two-week exploration of Cartagena, where you'll encounter a captivating blend of history, beauty, and cultural diversity. Let's dive into the itinerary:

Days 1 - 3: Unveiling Old Town's Enchanting Wonders

Begin your adventure in the mesmerizing Old Town. Lose yourself in its labyrinthine cobblestone streets adorned with vibrant colonial buildings. Immerse yourself in the city's rich heritage by visiting iconic landmarks such as the San Felipe Castle and the renowned Clock Tower. Don't forget to treat your taste buds to the local delights at cozy cafes tucked away in hidden corners.

Days 4 - 6: Getsemaní - Where Bohemian Vibes Thrive

Next, venture into Getsemaní, an eclectic neighborhood oozing with artistic charm. Allow yourself to be captivated by its colorful street art and immerse yourself in its vibrant markets. Feel the pulse of history as you explore significant sites like the Sanctuary of Saint Peter Claver.

Days 7 - 9: Coastal Bliss - Rosario Islands and Barú

Escape to paradise as you set foot on the nearby Rosario Islands for an idyllic island retreat. Bask in the sun on pristine beaches, snorkel amidst crystal-clear waters teeming with marine life, and surrender to pure relaxation. Return to mainland bliss and discover the wonders of Barú Peninsula. Unwind on Playa Blanca's breathtaking beaches, explore mystical mangrove swamps, and let this tropical haven rejuvenate your soul.

Days 10 - 12: Unearthing Hidden Gems - Manga Neighborhood and La Boquilla

Rediscover historical charm as you delve into Manga neighborhood's well-preserved mansions surrounded by leafy streets. Stumble upon hidden plazas and uncover local gems that showcase Cartagena's authentic character. Then, venture to La Boquilla, a coastal village celebrated for its Afro-Caribbean traditions. Immerse yourself in the vibrant culture and perhaps even try your hand at traditional fishing techniques.

Days 13 - 15: The Grand Finale - Reveling in Old Town's Splendor

As your journey nears its end, return to the heart of Cartagena - the Old Town. Spend your final days indulging in the city's cultural richness. Rediscover favorite spots that have left an indelible mark on your soul, relish exquisite culinary experiences at top-notch restaurants, and take leisurely sunset strolls along the majestic city walls. Raise a glass of Colombian rum to toast to the memories created during this extraordinary voyage through Cartagena.

This meticulously crafted itinerary guarantees an immersive and unforgettable experience in Cartagena. It allows you to unravel the city's historic treasures, explore vibrant neighborhoods, and revel in its coastal splendor over two captivating weeks. So pack your bags and get ready for an adventure like no other!

Are you ready to embark on a thrilling journey through the vibrant city of Cartagena? Let's dive into the world of adventure activities that await you in this historic destination.

1. Old Town Exploration - Cartagena Historic District:

Uncover the fascinating history of Cartagena as you wander down its enchanting cobbled streets in the Old Town. Marvel at the awe-inspiring Castillo San Felipe de Barajas and soak in the breathtaking panoramic views from the Convento de la Popa.

2. Coastal Cycling - Bocagrande and Castillogrande:

Get on your bike and set off along the picturesque coastline of Cartagena, pedaling your way through the scenic beaches of Bocagrande and Castillogrande. Immerse yourself in the city's mesmerizing architecture and vibrant street life as you embark on this exhilarating cycling adventure.

3. Water Sports - Playa Blanca and Cartagena Beaches:

Plunge into the crystal-clear waters of Playa Blanca, where a vibrant underwater world awaits your exploration. Try your hand at windsurfing on Cartagena's pristine beaches, feeling the gentle breeze caress your face as you glide across azure waters.

4. Island Hopping and Sailing - Rosario Islands:

Escape to paradise by embarking on a day filled with island hopping and sailing around the breathtaking Rosario Islands. Dive into pristine waters, unwind on white-sand beaches, and immerse yourself in the beauty of Cartagena's maritime landscape.

5. Rock Climbing and Historical Trails - Castillo San Felipe de Barajas and La Popa Convent:

Combine adrenaline-pumping rock climbing with a touch of history as you conquer Castillo San Felipe de Barajas, an iconic fortress that offers unparalleled views. For a truly unique experience, venture to La Popa Convent, where challenging rock-climbing routes intertwine with a rich historical backdrop.

6. White-Water Adventures - Sinú River:

Embark on a thrilling white-water adventure along the Sinú River, where you can indulge in heart-pounding activities like rafting and kayaking amidst lush landscapes. Feel the rush of adrenaline as you navigate through the rapids, surrounded by nature's beauty.

To make the most of your adventures in Cartagena, here are the best times to visit:

- November to March: Perfect for hiking and cycling, as temperatures are cooler during these months.
- April to June: Ideal for water sports and sailing enthusiasts, with warm Caribbean waters inviting you to dive right in.
- July to October: Explore historical sites and challenge yourself with rock climbing during these months.

Cartagena's diverse landscapes and historical sites offer an array of exhilarating activities. Whether you're immersing yourself in ancient forts, embarking on a coastal cycling expedition, or diving into the turquoise waters of the Caribbean Sea, each adventure in Cartagena promises a unique blend of history and natural beauty. Get ready to create memories that will last a lifetime!

Cartagena, Colombia, has a captivating history that dates back to the indigenous cultures that once thrived in the region before European explorers arrived. These tribes, such as the Karib and Arawak, left their mark on the land known as Calamari.

In 1501, Spanish explorer Rodrigo de Bastidas became the first European to set foot in this area. However, it wasn't until 1533 when Spanish conquistador Pedro de Heredia founded Cartagena. The indigenous population fiercely resisted the Spanish intrusion, but ultimately, the settlement took hold and became an important outpost for the Spanish Crown.

As Cartagena grew in importance, it also became a target for pirates and privateers who sought to plunder its wealth. Notable figures like Sir Francis Drake and John Hawkins attempted to sack the city, leading to the construction of strong fortifications.

To defend against maritime raids, defensive structures were built under orders from the Spanish Crown. One of these structures is the iconic San Felipe de Barajas Castle, completed in the mid-17th century. It served as a symbol of Cartagena's determination to resist external threats.

During colonial times, Cartagena played a significant role in the transatlantic slave trade. The city's port was a major arrival point for African slaves who were forcibly brought to work on plantations and mines in America. Today, Afro-Caribbean cultural influences can still be seen in Cartagena's vibrant music, dance, and cuisine.

Despite hardships faced by enslaved individuals during this period, Cartagena flourished economically and became one of Spain's wealthiest ports within its empire. This prosperity is reflected in its grand architecture including opulent churches and cobbled streets.

In early 19th century Latin America independence movements swept through various territories including Cartagena which declared independence from Spain on November 11th 1811 becoming one of first territories to do so. However, it was not an easy journey.

1815 witnessed the Battle of Cartagena, a significant event in the fight for independence. Spanish forces led by General Pablo Morillo besieged the city for months. Despite enduring a harsh blockade and bombardment, the residents of Cartagena remained determined to resist. In 1816, however, Spanish forces ultimately took control temporarily thwarting aspirations for independence.

After Colombia gained independence from Spain in 1819, Cartagena faced political and economic challenges as power shifted between different factions. Additionally, with the opening of Panama Canal in early 20th century, the city's strategic importance as a port diminished leading to economic decline.

The political landscape during this time was tumultuous and marked by tragedy such as the assassination of liberal leader Rafael Nuñez in 1894. These events highlighted the persistent political tensions within Colombia during this period.

Despite these challenges, Cartagena experienced a cultural renaissance in the 20th century. Efforts to preserve its historical architecture gained momentum resulting in UNESCO declaring its historic center as a World Heritage Site in 1984. This recognition brought international attention to Cartagena's architectural treasures and boosted tourism while nurturing a renewed sense of pride in its heritage.

As a result of being recognized as a UNESCO World Heritage Site, extensive restoration projects were undertaken to ensure that Cartagena's colonial charm is preserved. Today, the walled city stands as living proof of its people's resilience and their commitment to safeguard their cultural legacy.

Cartagena's transformation from economic decline to a thriving hub of tourism and commerce in the latter half of the 20th century is a testament to its modern era. The city capitalized on its historical significance, attracting visitors from around the world with its well-preserved architecture and cultural heritage.

The restoration of colonial-era mansions into boutique hotels, the development of luxury resorts, and the promotion of Cartagena's cultural festivals played a significant role in its resurgence.

Notably, the Hay Festival, an international literary gathering, showcased Cartagena's intellectual and artistic contributions.

Cartagena's strategic location on the Caribbean coast and its cultural richness made it a sought-after destination for history enthusiasts as well as those seeking sun-soaked beaches, vibrant nightlife, and Colombian hospitality.

Diverse influences have shaped Cartagena's rich cultural tapestry throughout history. The city's music reflects a fusion of indigenous, African, and European traditions with genres like cumbia and vallenato taking center stage. The annual Cartagena Music Festival celebrates this diversity and showcases the city's vibrant culture.

Afro-Caribbean influences are particularly prominent in Cartagena's culinary scene with dishes like sancocho and arepas reflecting African heritage. Traditional dances such as Mapalé showcase the rhythmic expressions rooted in Afro-Caribbean culture.

While thriving as a tourist destination, Cartagena faces common challenges found in urban centers such as inequality, infrastructure development, and climate change impact on coastal areas. However, Cartagena has always been resilient throughout history and continues to navigate these challenges towards sustainable growth.

In the 21st century, Cartagena strikes a balance between modern development and preserving its historical treasures. The lively energy permeating through its streets filled with street vendors' sounds, musicians' melodies, laughter from locals and tourists alike is a testament to its enduring spirit.

Cartagena has experienced a tourism boom in recent years, attracting a diverse array of travelers. Its well-preserved colonial architecture, luxurious resorts, and thriving culinary scene make it a popular destination for history enthusiasts and relaxation seekers. High-profile events like international film festivals and fashion shows have further elevated Cartagena's global recognition.

Cartagena's international acclaim goes beyond its historical significance; it has become a symbol of Colombian resilience and cultural pride. Visitors are not only invited to explore the cobblestone streets and historic fortifications but also to immerse themselves in the vibrant cultural tapestry that defines Cartagena today.

As Cartagena embraces modern urban life, there is a concerted effort to ensure sustainable and inclusive growth. Preservation initiatives protect the architectural gems of the historic center, while urban planning aims to address the needs of the local population.

The commitment to sustainable tourism is evident through environmental conservation initiatives and responsible travel practices. Balancing economic progress with the preservation of natural and cultural heritage remains a top priority as Cartagena looks towards the future.

In conclusion, Cartagena is not just a relic of the past but a living chronicle that continues to evolve. From its indigenous roots and colonial struggles to its modern renaissance, Cartagena embodies resilience, diversity, and enduring spirit - characteristics that define the Colombian people.

Here are some amazing hotels in Cartagena, Bolivar, Colombia that you should consider for your stay:

1. Hotel Charleston Santa Teresa
   - Located at Carrera 3 31-23, this hotel offers a unique and captivating experience.
   - You can reach them at +57 5 6649494.
   - For more information, visit their website at [charlestonhotels.com](https://www.charlestonhotels.com/santa-teresa).

2. Casa San Agustin Hotel
   - Situated in Centro, Calle de la Universidad No. 36-44, this hotel promises luxury and comfort.
   - Feel free to contact them at +57 5 681 0000.
   - To explore further details, check out their website [hotelcasasanagustin.com](https://www.hotelcasasanagustin.com/).

3. Sofitel Legend Santa Clara Cartagena
   - Experience elegance and grandeur at Calle Del Torno 39-29 with this remarkable hotel.
   - You can reach them at +57 5 6504700.
   - Find out more about their offerings on their website [sofitel.accor.com](https://sofitel.accor.com/hotel/1871/index.en.shtml).

4. Hyatt Regency Cartagena
   - Located at Carrera 1 12-118, this hotel offers a perfect blend of luxury and convenience.
   - For inquiries or reservations, contact them at +57 5 6941234.
   - To learn more about what they have to offer, visit their website cartagena.regency.hyatt.com.

5. Casa Pestagua Hotel Boutique Spa
   - Discover tranquility and relaxation at Calle de Santo Domingo No. 33-63 with this exquisite hotel.

- Feel free to reach out to them at +57 5 6649494.
  - To explore their services and amenities, visit their website [hotelpestagua.com](https://www.hotelpestagua.com/).
6. Movich Hotel Cartagena de Indias
  - Experience luxury and comfort at Calle Velez Danies 33 136 with this exceptional hotel.
  - For inquiries or reservations, contact them at +57 5 6931000.
  - Learn more about their offerings on their website [movichhotels.com](https://movichhotels.com/en/cartagena/movich-hotel-cartagena/).
7. Hotel Caribe Cartagena
  - Located at Carrera 1 2-87, this hotel offers a delightful and memorable stay experience.
  - You can reach them at +57 5 6656200.
  - Find out more about their services on their website [hotelcaribe.com](https://www.hotelcaribe.com/).
8. Ananda Hotel Boutique
  - Immerse yourself in luxury and charm at Calle del Cuartel No.36-77 with this enchanting hotel.
  - Feel free to contact them at +57 5 6643220.
  - Explore further details on their website [anandacartagena.com](https://www.anandacartagena.com/).
9. Hotel Quadrifolio
  - Located at Calle del Cuartel 36-118, this hotel offers elegance and sophistication in every aspect.
  - For inquiries or reservations, contact them at +57 5 6605970.
   Visit their website quadrifoliohotel.com for more information.

These hotels provide excellent accommodation options and ensure a memorable stay in Cartagena, Bolivar, Colombia.

When planning a trip to Cartagena, it is important to understand the visa and residency regulations. This comprehensive guide will provide you with all the information you need:

1. Entry for European Citizens:

   - European citizens from countries that have agreements with Colombia can enter Cartagena using a valid identity card or passport.

2. Visa Exemptions for Select Countries:

   - Many countries, including the United States, Canada, Australia, and numerous European nations, often do not require visas for short-term visits. However, it is essential to check the specific requirements based on your nationality.

3. Visas for Non-Colombian Nationals:

   - Non-Colombian nationals who plan to visit Cartagena for purposes other than tourism (such as work or study) may need specific visas.

   - For the most accurate and up-to-date information, it is recommended to visit the official website of the Colombian Ministry of Foreign Affairs or contact your nearest Colombian consulate.

4. Residence and Work for Expatriates:

   - Expatriates who intend to live and work in Cartagena may need to obtain appropriate visas and permits.

   - Depending on their purpose of stay, individuals may be required to provide evidence of employment, a work contract, or sufficient financial means to support themselves.

5. Permanent Residence for Foreign Citizens:

   - Foreign citizens who have legally resided in Colombia continuously for a specified period may be eligible to apply for permanent residence status. The requirements for this status can vary, so it is advisable to consult with immigration authorities.

Cédula de Extranjería (Foreigner ID):

- Non-Colombian citizens planning an extended stay in Cartagena may need to obtain a 'Cédula de Extranjería' or Foreigner ID card.

- The application process involves dealing with immigration authorities, and specific documents may be required. The Cédula is necessary for various activities such as opening a bank account or signing a lease.

Study Visas:

- Non-Colombian students who wish to enroll in educational institutions in Cartagena must apply for a study visa.

- The application typically requires proof of enrollment, payment of tuition fees, and evidence of financial means to support oneself during the study period.

Understanding these intricacies of visas and residency is crucial for a smooth and compliant stay in Cartagena. It is recommended to consult official sources or seek guidance from local immigration offices to ensure you have accurate and updated information tailored to your specific situation.

When it comes to traveling to Cartagena, there are various transportation options available that provide convenience for travelers from different parts of the world. The city's rich history and vibrant culture make it an enticing destination.

By Air:

One of the main entry points to Cartagena is the Rafael Núñez International Airport. While it may not have as many intercontinental flights as larger cities, it still offers connectivity to major destinations. A mix of international and local airlines ensures a diverse range of flight options.

Entering the Country:

It's important to note that entry requirements can vary, so visitors should check specific regulations based on their nationality. Regardless, having a passport or ID card is mandatory, as these documents are essential for police registration upon hotel check-in.

By Land:

Cartagena has well-connected roads, buses, and rail systems that facilitate land travel to neighboring regions. There are land borders with Venezuela to the east and Panama to the northwest. When crossing these borders, thorough checks are conducted, so travelers should ensure they have all necessary documents.

By Bus:

For those looking for a cost-effective option, buses are available with varying levels of comfort and frequency. Local and regional bus services connect Cartagena with cities like Barranquilla and Santa Marta.

By Car and Motorcycle:

If you prefer driving or riding a motorcycle, there are a few things to keep in mind. Vehicles must display their nationality plates, and proof of vehicle ownership as well as third-party insurance is mandatory. The scenic roads in Cartagena make motorcycle touring popular, especially during the dry season.

By Train:

While train travel within Colombia is limited at present, there may be future developments in this area. However, for domestic travel within Colombia currently, most people opt for the extensive bus network instead.

By Sea:

Given its coastal location, sea travel is an enticing option when visiting Cartagena. The port serves as a hub for cruise ships, providing a picturesque arrival experience. Additionally, there are local ferry services that connect nearby islands, offering the opportunity for island-hopping adventures.

Understanding the diverse transportation options available ensures a smooth journey to Cartagena, allowing visitors to explore its wonders with ease. It's always advisable to check the latest travel advisories and entry requirements for a hassle-free experience.